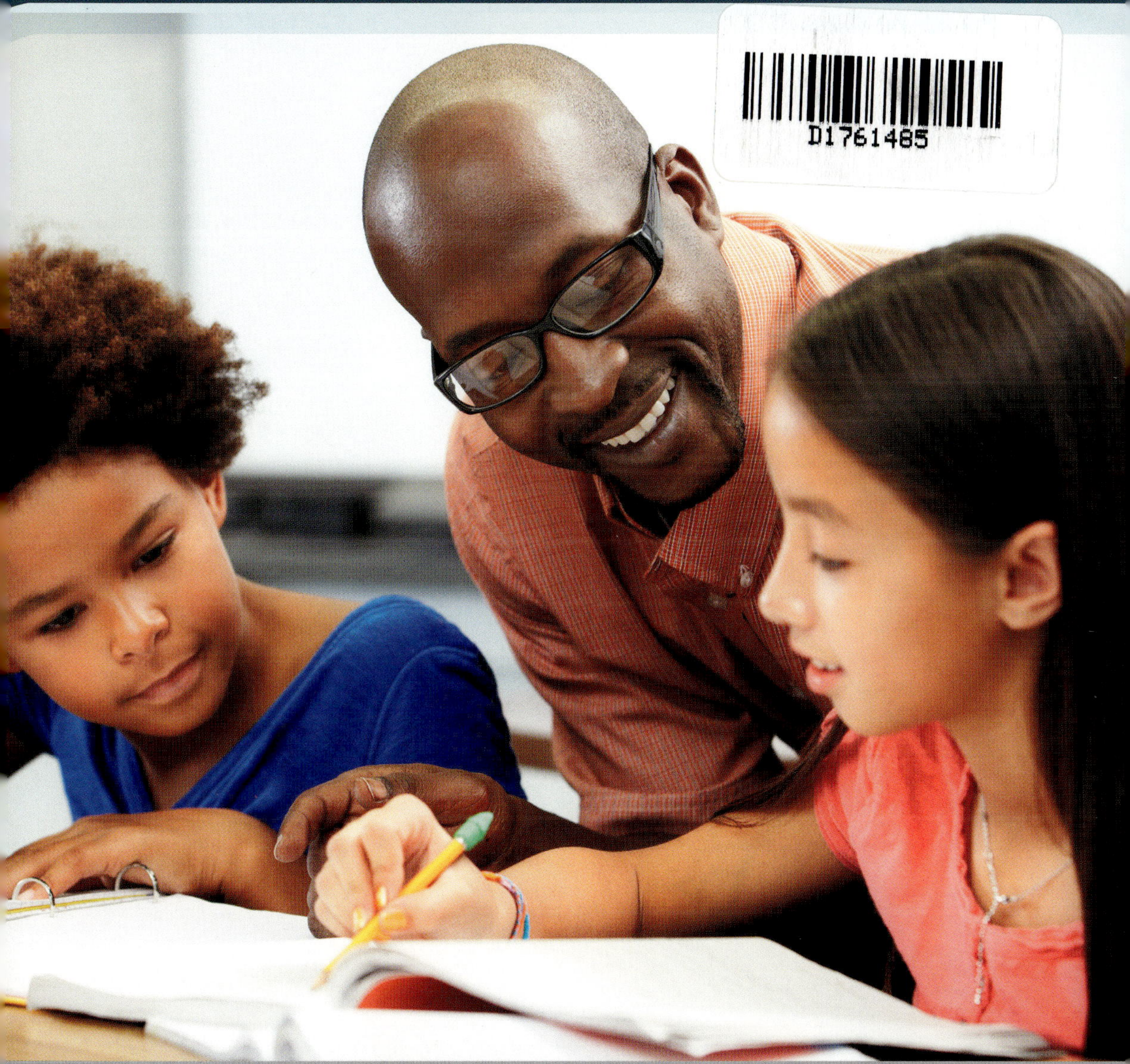

WORKING IN EDUCATION

by Marguerite A. Kistler

www.12StoryLibrary.com

Copyright © 2018 by 12-Story Library, Mankato, MN 56003. All rights reserved. No part of this book may be reproduced or utilized in any form or by any means without written permission from the publisher.

12-Story Library is an imprint of Bookstaves and Press Room Editions

Produced for 12-Story Library by Red Line Editorial

Photographs ©: Monkey Business Images/Shutterstock Images, cover, 1, 13, 19, 21, 22; DGLimages/Shutterstock Images, 4, 28; kali9/iStockphoto, 5; Rawpixel.com/Shutterstock Images, 6, 29; Tom Wang/Shutterstock Images, 7; l i g h t p o e t/Shutterstock Images, 8; monkeybusinessimages/iStockphoto, 9; Syda Productions/Shutterstock Images, 10; SpeedKingz/Shutterstock Images, 11; wavebreakmedia/Shutterstock Images, 12; FangXiaNuo/iStockphoto, 14; fstop123/iStockphoto, 15; vgajic/iStockphoto, 16; asiseeit/iStockphoto, 17, 27; FatCamera/iStockphoto, 18; XiXinXing/iStockphoto, 20; Fertnig/iStockphoto, 23; Tyler Olson/Shutterstock Images, 24; Klubovy/iStockphoto, 25; Izabela Habur/iStockphoto, 26

Library of Congress Cataloging-in-Publication Data
Names: Kistler, Marguerite A., author.
Title: Working in education / by Marguerite A. Kistler.
Description: Mankato, MN : 12 Story Library, [2017] | Series: Career Files |
  Includes bibliographical references and index. | Audience: Grades: 4 to 6.
Identifiers: LCCN 2016047400 (print) | LCCN 2017006068 (ebook) | ISBN
  9781632354433 (hardcover : alk. paper) | ISBN 9781632355102 (paperback :
  alk. paper) | ISBN 9781621435624 (hosted e-book)
Subjects: LCSH: Education--Vocational guidance--United States--Juvenile
  literature.
Classification: LCC LB1775.2 .K57 2017 (print) | LCC LB1775.2 (ebook) | DDC
  370.23/73--dc23
LC record available at https://lccn.loc.gov/2016047400

Printed in the United States of America
022017

Access free, up-to-date content on this topic plus a full digital version of this book. Scan the QR code on page 31 or use your school's login at 12StoryLibrary.com.

Table of Contents

There Are Many Choices in Education … 4

What Makes a Great Teacher? … 6

Teachers Learn How to Teach in School … 8

What Do Teachers Do? … 10

PE Teachers Get Kids Moving … 12

Report to the Principal's Office … 14

STEM Teachers Prepare Students for the Future … 16

Teachers Meet Students' Special Needs … 18

Aides and Paraprofessionals Provide Classroom Support … 20

ELL Teachers Help Students Understand the Language … 22

Library Media Specialists Teach Students about Information … 24

Teachers Look to the Future … 26

Other Jobs to Consider … 28

Glossary … 30

For More Information … 31

Index … 32

About the Author … 32

There Are Many Choices in Education

A career in education can mean teaching music in a preschool or math in college. Teaching any subject can be part of an education career. But it's not just about being in a classroom. Education includes principals and librarians. Teachers at museums and coaches are also types of educators.

Teachers can work with any age group. Early childhood educators are always needed. These educators work with preschool children. School children and teens also need teachers. And professors teach in colleges. Educators can also work outside the formal school system. Some people provide training for adults who want to start a new job or learn new job skills. And teachers in community education programs offer classes to adult learners of all ages.

Educators can pursue their careers anywhere in the world. Teachers are needed in small towns and huge cities. Every country on earth needs teachers.

Early childhood educators are in demand.

Teachers can change paths partway through their careers. They don't have to do the same thing until they retire. Some teachers enjoy spending many years teaching the same subject. Others switch to something different as their interests change. They might begin as a fourth-grade teacher. Then they might decide to teach English in China. They could teach preschool. Then they might choose to become a reading specialist. People who want to work in education have many options.

3.7 million
Number of teachers in US schools in 2014.

- Educators can work in a variety of settings, including classrooms, museums, or athletic fields.
- Different types of educators work with learners of all ages.
- Teachers are needed all over the world.

Field trip tour guides are educators, too.

What Makes a Great Teacher?

Teachers are expected to be patient with the students in their classrooms. Students may not understand concepts and ideas the first time they are presented. It takes time to master a new skill.

Educators must understand their students' needs. They plan lessons to teach the same idea in many ways. Students have different learning styles. For example, some students are visual learners. They understand ideas through images and pictures. Teachers must adapt their lessons to their students' different learning styles. Teachers assess, or test, students. Testing helps educators know which students need more help. Other students may be ready to work on harder lessons. Educators must keep good records of each student's progress.

Teachers often work with other educators. They work as a team to help students. Teachers also call or meet with parents to discuss their students' learning.

Teachers may plan hands-on activities to keep students engaged.

Great teachers know how to make learning new concepts fun.

Great teachers go beyond lessons, testing, and teamwork. They take time to know their students. They show concern for them. Great educators explain lessons in ways that help each student understand them. These lessons get students excited to learn more. Great teachers make learning fun.

Educators need to keep learning, too. They study the subjects they teach. Great teachers also study new ways to teach their students.

$57,200
Average salary of a high school teacher in the United States in 2015.

- Teachers need to be patient while their students learn new skills and concepts.
- Teachers must plan lessons that meet the needs of students with different learning styles.
- Great teachers always continue learning new ways to teach their students.

TEACHERS IN DEMAND

There is a shortage of teachers in the United States. However, there are some teachers that are needed even more. Almost all states reported a shortage of special education teachers in 2016. Schools are also looking for math, science, and technology teachers. Openings for educators who can teach English language learners are growing as well.

3

Teachers Learn How to Teach in School

Most states require teachers to earn a license before they can start teaching. But there are different requirements for teaching younger or older students. Different kinds of teachers need different training.

Teachers usually spend four years in college earning a bachelor's degree. They take classes on the history of education. They learn about the best ways to teach students. Teachers study the age group they will teach. They need to know how a kindergartener's brain is different from a middle-schooler's brain. They learn how to assess students and study ways to help students learn.

Educators take extra classes in the areas they would like to specialize in. A science teacher needs extra science courses.

TEACHERS IN SCHOOL

Some teachers take one or two more years of college classes to earn an advanced degree. This degree is called a master's degree. On average, a special education teacher with a bachelor's degree earns $56,800 each year in the United States. A teacher with a master's degree earns an average of $62,270.

Most people attend college before becoming teachers.

10

Minimum number of weeks the National Council on Teacher Quality says student teaching experiences should last.

- Many states require teachers to be licensed.
- Most teachers have a bachelor's degree.
- In college, education students choose the subject and age level they want to teach.
- Before completing their degree, education students spend time in a classroom student teaching.

THINK ABOUT IT

Why is student teaching important? What might student teachers learn during this time? What might be hardest for them?

After graduating, teachers continue to take classes to stay knowledgeable about current education practices.

Special education teachers must take classes about students with special needs.

During the last year of college, most education students teach in a school. This is sometimes called student teaching. They watch what the teachers do and teach classes of their own. The classroom teachers help when needed.

9

4
What Do Teachers Do?

Students in classrooms are very different from one another. Some learn quickly. Others need extra help. Still others might have physical challenges. Educators find ways to help each student do his or her best.

Teachers must help their students learn the concepts required for their grade level. Learning guidelines, or standards, for each subject are chosen by each state. These guidelines help teachers know what should be taught. Many hours are spent preparing lessons and materials to teach these concepts.

Tests and quizzes help teachers know which students need more practice on these concepts. Each spring, many states require students to take exams in English, math, and science. The results of these assessments show when schools and students are succeeding.

Educators must communicate with each child's family members. Teachers give them important

Test results let teachers know what their students need more help with.

Some teachers teach extra subjects, such as drama, after the school day ends.

information about their child's learning. Teachers are also responsible for meeting the requirements of their principal and school district.

Many teachers take on responsibilities beyond their classrooms. They might lead a chess, drama, or writing club. Some organize science fairs or teach in after-school or summer programs. Others coach sports teams.

CLASS SIZES

Class sizes are different in urban, suburban, and rural schools. An average urban middle school class has 30 students. Suburban classes average 27 students. And there is an average of 21 students in rural schools.

53
Average number of hours that teachers in the United States work during each week of school.

- Teachers must help students learn the concepts required for their grade level.
- State testing helps show when schools and students are succeeding.
- Communication with students' family members is an important part of a teacher's job.
- Some teachers also coach sports or lead after-school clubs.

5
PE Teachers Get Kids Moving

Physical education (PE) teachers show students how to include a healthy amount of physical activity in their lives. PE teachers do many of the same tasks as classroom teachers. They plan lessons carefully to meet the needs of all students. They also assess students and help them do their best.

PE teachers plan lessons about many different types of physical activity. They teach students about the benefits of each activity. PE classes often include sports and games. Some schools use swimming pools for PE class. They might use jump ropes and climbing walls as well.

PE teachers can also help students learn how to meditate and stay calm.

PE teachers plan their lessons around the national standards. PE classes for kindergarteners might include basic motor skills, such as hopping, galloping, and balance. As students get older, PE lessons will focus on more complex skills and activities, such as dribbling a basketball or hitting a ball with a baseball bat.

In addition to teaching their classes, PE teachers often coach sports teams at their schools. Large schools have many sports teams. Each team needs a coach.

Coaches must know the sport they are coaching very well. They teach special skills for each sport.

150
Number of minutes of PE class recommended per week for first through fifth grade students.

- In PE classes, students learn how to be physically active.
- PE classes include many different types of physical activities.
- PE teachers plan lessons that help their students meet the national PE standards.

Coaches also plan for games against other teams. Working with parents is an important part of coaching.

A PE teacher might double as a basketball coach.

13

Report to the Principal's Office

School principals must have good leadership skills. They are ultimately responsible for what happens in all classrooms at their school. Principals work with students, teachers, and parents. They are responsible to school district leaders.

Principals first go to college for four years to become a teacher. Most principals must teach for at least two years before becoming principals. In addition to this teaching experience, principals also need to have a master's degree. This means they go to college for two more years.

Principals observe teachers and classes. Principals suggest ways teachers can improve. School testing is especially important to principals. They look closely at scores and

Good principals get to know the students in their schools.

Principals help make sure teachers and parents are on the same page.

find ways to improve their school's performance. Principals help students work hard. They work with students who have gotten into trouble. Principals meet with students, parents, and teachers to discuss classroom behavior and make plans for the future.

Principals also attend important meetings, such as budget meetings. Each school receives only a certain amount of money each year. Principals decide how that money is spent.

$90,410
Average salary for a principal in a US school.

- Principals are ultimately responsible for everything that happens at their school.
- Principals must have both teaching experience and a master's degree.
- Principals work to improve the education students receive at their schools.

THINK ABOUT IT

Why do you think it is important for principals to be teachers first? How might this help them be better principals? Why do they observe classrooms?

7

STEM Teachers Prepare Students for the Future

In 2015, there were 8.6 million US jobs in science, technology, engineering, and math (STEM). That number keeps growing larger year after year. To help students prepare for these jobs, schools need STEM teachers. Schools want to give students the training they need.

Some schools begin STEM subjects in preschool. Starting in kindergarten, science and math are taught in every grade. Some schools also incorporate technology into lessons on a variety of subjects. Public schools in the United States provide at least one computer for every five students.

One way educators help students develop STEM skills is by putting on science fairs. At these events, students choose a STEM topic to investigate. Working on these projects helps students learn how scientists find answers to scientific questions. This gets students excited about STEM.

Schools are offering coding classes to younger and younger students.

16

$3 billion
Amount of money spent each year on digital materials for US schools.

- Jobs in STEM are on the rise.
- STEM teachers help students prepare for these jobs.
- Educators help students relate science to their daily lives.

INTEL ISEF

Some high school students enter regional and state science fair competitions. Those that do can earn a spot to present at the Intel International Science and Engineering Fair (ISEF). ISEF awards more than $4 million each year to fund additional experiments by new and budding scientists. For example, Kathy Liu of Utah won $50,000 in 2016 to research her ideas on alternative battery parts.

STEM teachers help students gain interest in STEM by teaching them to relate those subjects to their daily lives. For example, educators might use gaming to teach computer and math skills. Or they might help students connect science concepts to current events in the news.

Educational video games can be used to teach complex STEM topics.

8

Teachers Meet Students' Special Needs

Some students have special needs. They learn differently. Or they might have a disability that affects their ability to learn. Educators who teach these students are called special education teachers. They are trained to meet these students' educational needs. Special education teachers are required to have bachelor's degree. Some educators major in special education. In addition, some states require a master's degree. All of this coursework teaches educators the best ways to help students with special needs.

Special education teachers help to develop an individualized education program (IEP) for each student. The plan lists goals for the student and tells how the student and teacher will work together. Educators track the student's learning. Teachers and parents meet to discuss the plans. Changes are made if needed.

Some students need help with physical disabilities. For example,

Speech educators often meet with students one on one.

Special education teachers meet with students and parents to plan an IEP that works for everyone.

Speech and Language educators help students learn to speak clearly and correctly. Students who do not hear well may have a special device to make the teacher's voice louder.

Autistic students need help with behaviors, language, and relationships. Some students struggle with strong emotions. Educators help them learn ways to control their emotions and stay calm. Some students need help all day. Others only need these services for part of the day.

The need for special education teachers is growing. More students are being diagnosed with special needs. As a result, more special education teachers will be needed in the future.

6.5 million
Number of students in the United States who receive special education services.

- Special education teachers require special training on the best ways to help students with special needs.
- An IEP lists educational goals based on a student's needs.
- Special education teachers might help students with a wide variety of special needs, such as physical disabilities or autism.

9
Aides and Paraprofessionals Provide Classroom Support

Classroom teachers sometimes need help for students with special needs. This help is given by teachers' assistants. These aides and paraprofessionals work with teachers to meet the needs of their students.

An aide does not need to have taken any college classes. Paraprofessionals usually need to have completed two years of college or have an associate's degree. However, *aide* and *paraprofessional* are often used to describe any teacher's assistant. An assistant is not the child's teacher but is there to help the student understand what is being taught.

Some aides help the same student all day. For example, a student who has trouble moving around needs help getting on and off the bus, getting outside at recess, and navigating the lunchroom. Aides also help these students during classroom activities.

Sometimes aides work with a few students in the same class. For example, an aide may move from student to student checking their work. Students with behavioral

An aide might accompany his or her assigned student to the cafeteria.

THINK ABOUT IT

What character traits might be important for aides? What are some other ways aides can help students?

1.2 million
Number of aides working in the United States.

- Many aides do not need college degrees.
- Aides and paraprofessionals are supervised by teachers.
- Some aides work with one student full time, while others work with a few different students.
- Aides provide students with the support they need to meet their education goals.

challenges will be reminded to use good behavior. Others will have directions repeated or explained. For those who have trouble focusing, the aide helps them stay on task.

Aides work to help students become as independent as possible. They work closely with teachers to make sure students reach their IEP goals. Parents are kept informed of their child's progress. New tasks can be hard. Aides help with these new tasks. They encourage students to keep trying. Aides give them only the help they need. Then students can do more and more on their own.

Aides help students learn by checking in with them during class.

10

ELL Teachers Help Students Understand the Language

Many schools in the United States have students who did not learn English at home. Their parents speak a different language. When these students come to school, they need help learning English in addition to learning all other subjects. Their teachers are called English language learner (ELL) teachers.

ELL teachers test students to see how much English they understand. Then the teachers plan lessons and activities. One goal is to increase the students' level of understanding and use of English. ELL teachers also try to introduce some American traditions and culture.

ELL teachers may have students from many different countries. The teachers do not need to know all the languages. However, they must understand and respect the differences of each culture.

ELL educators are a bridge between the school and students' family members. They help families understand what their children are expected to do. They may also help classroom teachers and students interact with English language learners.

ELL teachers must be able to communicate with kids who speak many different languages.

ELL teachers meet with parents and work with them to help students learn.

ELL teachers generally need to go to college for four years. They earn a bachelor's degree and a teaching certificate. Some states require teachers to earn a TESOL (teachers of English to speakers of other languages) certificate.

TEACHING AT MILITARY SCHOOLS

Some educators can find jobs at schools in foreign countries where the students speak English. The US Department of Defense has schools around the world. These schools are for children of military families. Other students may also go there. These teachers are required to have the same teaching degrees as in the United States.

4.5 million

Number of students in the United States in ELL programs.

- Children who did not learn English at home are assisted by ELL teachers.
- ELL teachers do not have to understand the languages students speak at home, but they do need to respect different cultures.
- ELL teachers can help families understand what their children need to learn at school.
- Bachelor's degrees are required for ELL teachers.

11
Library Media Specialists Teach Students about Information

School librarians, or library media specialists, build collections. These can include books, magazines, CDs, and computers.

Librarians organize educational materials so they're easy for students to find.

It is the librarian's job to buy and organize these materials. Librarians also help students find the materials they need.

Librarians do not usually work in the classroom, but they still teach. They help students learn where to find information, both using books and digital resources. They might also read to elementary school students. Reading from a book gets students interested in it. Librarians teach students how to take care of the materials available in the library.

School librarians also help teachers. Teachers might need information for lessons. Librarians collect the materials for them.

Librarians help make sure the computer records for all library materials are accurate. Librarians

LIBRARY ASSISTANTS

A library assistant helps the librarian. The assistant keeps the library records in order. Some schools require an assistant to have a college degree. Others require only a high school diploma. This can be a full- or part-time job. Library assistants do not usually work during the summer. On average, library assistants in the United States earn $13.43 per hour.

54
Percentage of US librarians who work in education.

- School librarians teach students how to find information using the resources available in the library.
- Librarians also help teachers find resources for their lessons.
- Librarians manage all of the books and technology in the library.

also decide when materials are too outdated. These are removed from the shelves. Then librarians pick out new materials to replace them. Librarians decide how the library's money is spent.

Librarians also help students use reading rooms.

25

Teachers Look to the Future

Educators of the future may be trained in different ways. They will learn more about STEM teaching. Teachers will use new technology in their classrooms. It will be important to connect with educators and students around the world.

Teachers will need to help students use electronic devices. Some schools already loan tablets to students. Those students then send their assignments to their teachers electronically. Some teachers send students links to PowerPoint lessons, which can be downloaded. These lessons can be watched at home or at school. The electronic tablets are also used for research and student presentations.

Teachers also help students use technology to connect with those in other countries. Students use electronic tablets to create blogs and videos about

Technology such as virtual reality can now be used to teach STEM classes.

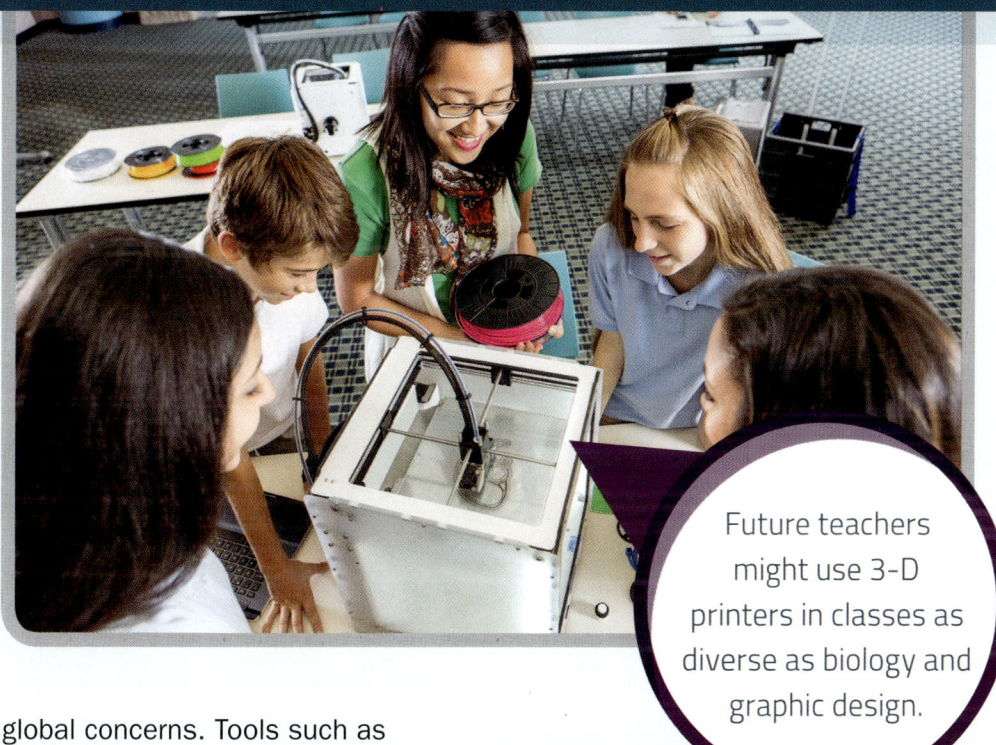

Future teachers might use 3-D printers in classes as diverse as biology and graphic design.

global concerns. Tools such as Skype make meetings with students around the world possible. For example, US students have talked with those in Bangalore, India, to understand environmental concerns. Students from classrooms in many countries are challenging one another to solve problems in a global engineering club.

New tools are being used at every grade level. For example, in some schools, kindergarteners learn enough coding to program a robot. Some high schools have fabrication labs. There, students design an item on the computer. Then they use a 3-D printer to actually create the item.

33
Percentage of US high school students who use mobile devices provided by their school.

- Some students and teachers use new electronics, such as tablets, in the classroom.
- Technology can also connect students and schools across the world, so they can work together on global problems.
- New tools are used at every grade level, from kindergarten to 12th grade.

Other Jobs to Consider

Preschool Teacher

Description: Teach students younger than five who have not yet entered kindergarten
Training/Education: Associate's degree
Outlook: Growing
Average salary: $28,570

High School Art Teacher

Description: Guide students in drawing, painting, ceramics, and art history
Training/Education: Bachelor's degree
Outlook: Growing
Average salary: $57,200

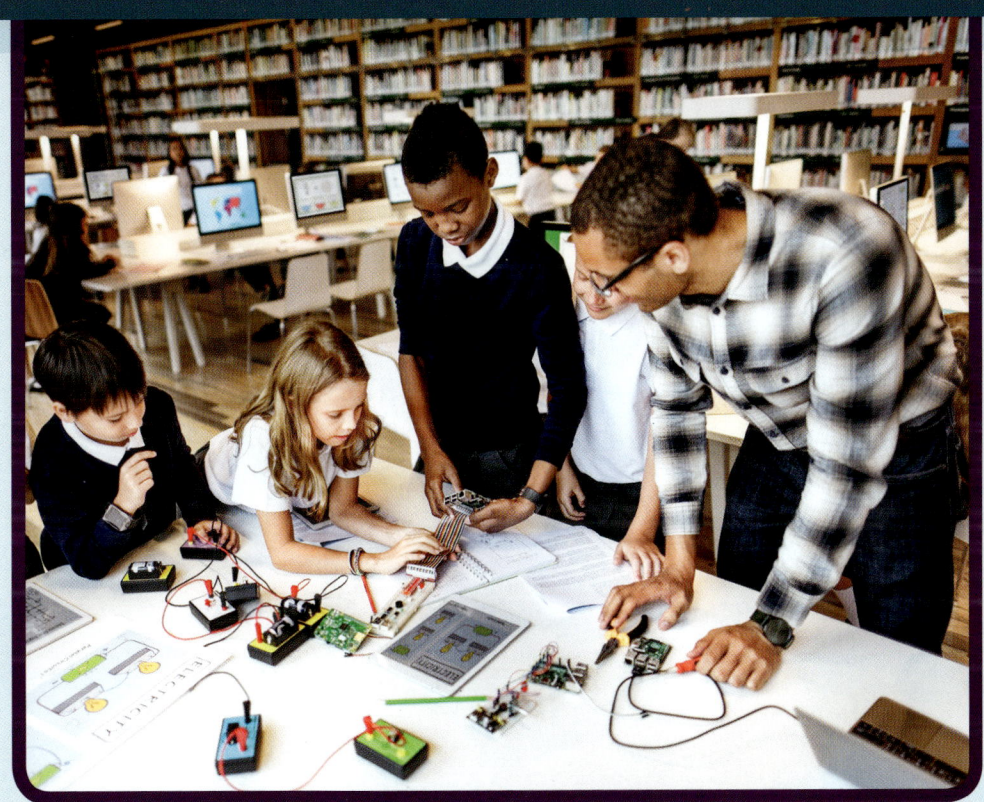

Guidance Counselor

Description: Help students develop school and social skills to succeed in school
Training/Education: Master's degree
Outlook: Growing
Average salary: $53,660

College Science Professor

Description: Prepare students for a career in science or medicine
Training/Education: Doctoral degree
Outlook: Growing
Average salary: $72,470

Glossary

assess
To judge the quality of something.

autism
A disability that can create social, behavioral, and physical challenges.

budget
A plan for how money will be spent.

concept
An idea.

disability
A condition that limits a person's ability to do something others do easily.

independent
To be able to control one's self.

individualized
Special for each person.

requirements
Items that are needed.

rural
In the countryside.

specialist
A person who studies a certain subject or occupation.

suburban
In a town close to a large city.

supervise
To oversee.

urban
In a large city.

For More Information

Books

Cohn, Jessica. *On the Job at School*. South Egremont, MA: Red Chair, 2016.

Silivanch, Annalise. *A Career as a Teacher*. New York: Rosen, 2011.

Sunseri, Sophia Natasha. *Working as a Teacher in Your Community*. New York: Rosen, 2016.

Visit 12StoryLibrary.com

Scan the code or use your school's login at **12StoryLibrary.com** for recent updates about this topic and a full digital version of this book. Enjoy free access to:

- Digital ebook
- Breaking news updates
- Live content feeds
- Videos, interactive maps, and graphics
- Additional web resources

Note to educators: Visit 12StoryLibrary.com/register to sign up for free premium website access. Enjoy live content plus a full digital version of every 12-Story Library book you own for every student at your school.

Index

aides, 20–21

bachelor's degree, 8, 18, 23

classroom teachers, 4, 6, 9, 10, 11, 14, 15, 20, 22, 26–27
coaches, 4, 13
college, 4, 8, 9, 14, 20, 23

English language learners, 7, 22–23

high school, 17, 25, 27

kindergarten, 8, 13, 16, 27

learning styles, 6
librarians, 4, 24–25
library assistants, 25

master's degree, 8, 14, 18
math teachers, 7, 16–17
middle school, 8, 11
military schools, 23

paraprofessionals, 20
physical education teachers, 12–13
preschool, 4, 5, 16
principals, 4, 14–15

science fairs, 11, 16, 17
science teachers, 7, 8, 16–17
special education teachers, 7, 8, 9, 18–19
speech and language educators, 19
STEM, 16–17, 26

technology teachers, 7, 16–17, 26–27
tests, 6, 7, 10, 14, 22

About the Author
Marguerite A. Kistler has taught high school English, second and first grades, and online writing courses for teens. She is a reading specialist and author in Pittsburgh, Pennsylvania.

READ MORE FROM 12-STORY LIBRARY

Every 12-Story Library book is available in many formats. For more information, visit 12StoryLibrary.com.